MW00624641

FAMILIUS

Published by Familius LLC, www.familius.com
Familius books are available at special discounts for
bulk purchases for sales promotions or for family or
corporate use. Special editions, including personalized
covers, excerpts of existing books, or books with corporate logos, can be created in large quantities for special
needs. For more information, contact Premium Sales at
559-876-2170 or email specialmarkets@familius.com.

Library of Congress Cataloging-in-Publication Data
2015956715
Print ISBN 9781942934424

Printed in China

Edited by Brooke Jorden
Cover design by David Miles
Book design by Brooke Jorden and David Miles

10 9 8 7 6 5 4 3 2 1

First Edition

MOTHER

ALWAYS KNOWS BEST
(AT LEAST ACCORDING TO HER)

175
Jokes
for the only angel that uses a whisk

GENE & LINDA PERRET

You know, Mom, I've known you all my life. In fact, when I was born, I think you were in the same hospital I was. You had to be, Mom, because you were always there for me. When I would wake up two or three times during the night bawling my eyes out, you were my nourishment. When I fell on my bottom so many times learning to walk, you were my pick-me-up. As a novice riding a bike, I would often fall and skin my knees. You were my first aid kit. When I'd get in trouble at school, you'd rush to my defense and then invariably take the teacher's side. When I was ill, nothing felt better than your caring hand on my forehead. (It was certainly better than some of the medicines you made me swallow.) You were there for me when I was happy and when I was sad. You loved me when I was pleasant and when I pouted. When I was tiny, you taught me to do what you told me to do. When I got older, you gave me the courage and the character to pursue my own dreams.

We've been through quite a bit together, you and I. Somehow I always wound up getting the better part of the deal. That's the way mothers are. They're giving, caring, unselfish, and loving.

You've given me so much more than I can ever repay. You presented me with the most precious gift of all—life itself.

This book says that Mom is always right. She always has been and always will be. Even those few times when she may have been wrong, she's been right (at least according to her). This book is a tender admission that despite the squabbles, conflicts, arguments, and disagreements, Mom was always right. We not only acknowledge that in these pages, but we thank her for it.

Through laughter, we share our love for Mom.

Gene Perret and Linda Perret

Mothers are angels
with the wings
removed . . .

It makes them
easier to hug.

Mother:

a person who loves
you even during
those times when no
one else would, could,
or should.

Mom—
the original lie
detector.

Mom could take
the most complex
situation and explain
it with one simple
sentence:

"Because i said so,
that's why."

Moms have such tender,
loving, caring hands . . .
unless they're brandishing a

wooden
spoon.

Only a mother
could spit on a
handkerchief, clean
your face with it,
and still be loved
afterward.

The doctor was the first person to spank my bottom.

Mom was the second, but she did it more frequently and more consistently.

When Mom says,

"Did you have a good time?"

it always sounds as though it should be followed by,

"Do you swear to tell the truth, the whole truth, and nothing but the truth . . . ?"

No matter how many candles you have on the cake, Mom always reminds you that "You're still not too old to be put over my knee."

A mother's kiss on a boo-boo—the original penicillin.

Mom always had strict dating rules; they were the same as the requirements for being accepted into a

BENEDICTINE MONASTERY.

Mom gets shorter as
she gets older.
That comes from years
and years of

putting her
foot down.

Mom could express
love with a

WARM HUG

or a

WHACK ON
THE HEAD.

Both worked, but one hurt
more than the other . . .
sometimes it was the hug.

Moms are the good cop of parenthood.

Some people call it a
"Jack-of-all-trades."

At our house, we
called that
" mom."

I asked my mother once if I was adopted. She said,

"SO FAR, NO."

Mom never let us keep strays.

Once i walked in the door and she said, "You take that thing to the pound this instant, do you hear me?"

i said, "Mom, this is my new **boyfriend.**"

Mom insisted that all
my dates had to first
meet the family and be

Mirandized.

Only a mother could give birth to her children, nourish them, protect them, nurse them through illnesses, educate them, encourage them, guide them, drive them here and there, and prepare them for a secure and productive life of their own . . . all while Dad read the newspaper.

Mom, do you remember
how i used to help you
with the dishes?

Neither do I.

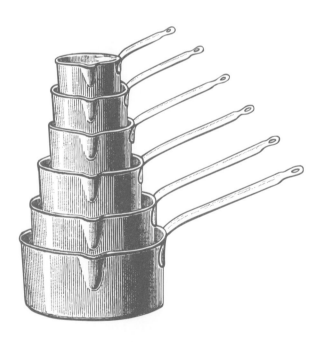

Mom was obsessed with cleanliness. She would

WASH THE SOAP

before she used it.

Mom kept all of us kids
so clean we always
thought we were

FOR SALE.

Mom was a
cleanliness freak.

I would be four inches
taller today if Mom
hadn't made me wipe
my feet so much.

Mom was adamant that
we always wash behind
our ears.

i don't know what exactly
went on behind my ears, but it
must have left a terrible mess.

We followed Mom's instructions, too. We kids were so proud of the back of our ears that when people took our picture, we faced

away from the camera.

Mom puts starch in everything.

My brother fell out of bed once and broke his **pajamas.**

Mom even starched our handkerchiefs. Have you ever tried to blow your nose with a

paper plate?

Mom would always say,

"Stop fighting. You're brother and sister, for crying out loud."

We assumed that Mom wasn't against fighting—she just preferred that we do it with strangers.

Mom had all kinds of
rules. God only had

TEN COMMANDMENTS.

Mom could never
have gotten by with
that few.

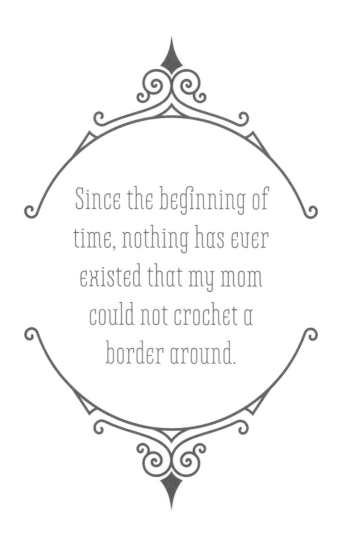

Since the beginning of time, nothing has ever existed that my mom could not crochet a border around.

Mom was
a stickler for
clean underwear.

in fact, all of her
children were
born wearing
clean underwear.

If I'm ever wanted by the FBI, the reward poster will read "Male, 6'1" tall, weighs 180 pounds, has anchor tattoo on left forearm, will be wearing

CLEAN
UNDERWEAR."

Mom said, "Always wear clean underwear in case you're in an accident." And it took.

Now, whenever I'm wearing clean underwear, I feel compelled to drive recklessly.

In fact, one year, that's what I wanted for Christmas—a pair of dirty underwear . . .

Santa said,

"i'll bring them, but you'd better drive carefully."

Mom asked, "Are you wearing clean underwear?" so often I started to wear my underwear on the

OUTSIDE.

That way she could tell just by looking.

Mom always insisted that no matter where I went, I had to wear clean underwear. It's one of the reasons why I never joined a

NUDIST COLONY.

I was born in a

taxi cab.

Even with the meter
running, Mom figured
it was cheaper than
a hospital room.

Mom could be tough.
She had a

BLACK BELT

in parenting.

Mom's parenting technique was a cross between Dr. Spock and Dr. Strangelove . . . with a generous helping of Rambo thrown in.

This'll give you an idea of
how strict Mom could be:
Her dress code for my
first date included a

suit of armor.

Mom could be rigid.
At parent-teacher
night, Mom would

INTIMIDATE

the other parents,
the teacher, the
principal, all of the
kids, and the Civil
War hero the school
was named after.

Mom is a genius with

COUPONS.

She can shop for her
weekly food allowance
and wind up with the
store owing her money.

Mom always wanted me to go to Notre Dame. When I asked why, she said,

"i have a coupon."

Mom was always good with money. That's the reason I got married.

Mom had a coupon at the **bridal shop.**

I honestly believe that if my mom ever had to hire a "hit man," she would have a coupon for it.

Mothers genuinely
love their children . . .
but then why does

"Someday you'll have
children of your own"

sound so much like
a threat?

Caterpillars transform into beautiful, delicate butterflies. How come it doesn't work that way when mothers transform into **mothers-in-law?**

Mom served leftovers four days a week.

That means that one day a week we had leftovers with no original meal attached.

Mom was always willing to give us advice. However, Mom's advice always ended with the words,

"OR ELSE."

Mom always volunteered at the church, taking on assignments that no one else would. She would do

anything

to get out of the house.

MOM,

we had many disagreements when I was a teenager, but not anymore.

You've learned so much since then.

Mom, when I was younger you protected me from doing things I shouldn't do. Thanks.

But I think you should know—I am doing a few of them now.

Mom and i have a lot in common. She ruled our household with an iron fist.

That's the same way i practiced my piano lessons.

Mom always knows best.

The real problem is that she knows that.

Moms always know what
their kids are doing.

Often, that's more than
their kids know.

Mom always knew best.
Mom was always right.
Mom always gave great advice.
Mom always had the last word.

And to this day, Mom
has no idea how

annoying

that can be.

Mom could be

FiERCE

with a wooden spoon.

Even when she just
used it for cooking, we
kids found ourselves
behaving better.

Mom had a tough
time raising us. Take
me, for example—my

"TERRIBLE TWOS"

lasted through my
third year of college.

Mom and I had many disagreements, but Mom always won.

It's hard to win an argument when your opponent is also the referee.

Mom spent an awful lot
of time driving us to

soccer
practice.

It took so long because
most of us didn't
want to go.

Mom felt that children should be seen and not heard. Eventually, she dropped the "seen" part, too.

A MOTHER'S KISS

is the most powerful medicine in the world.

A friend of mine went to medical school and he had a skeleton in his dorm room. His mom kissed it every time she left. After a couple of visits, its color started to come back.

Mom's kiss was so powerful at curing boo-boos that today you couldn't buy it over-the-counter.

Mom always told us to "wait one hour after eating before going into the water." I always believed that exactly one hour after eating I would sprout water wings.

To this day, I wait an hour after eating before filling the sink for shaving.

Mom would always question anyone we dated. Boy, was i glad when waterboarding was outlawed.

Funny thing about
dating—anytime we got

SERIOUS,

Mom got

GRIM.

Mom always found fault with anyone we dated. If I had dated Saint Augustine, Mom would have said,

"i hope he's not going to wear those silly sandals to the family picnic."

Mom put good meals on our table.

She felt it was a mother's duty to feed the mouths that argued with her.

Mom's motto was

"My way or the highway."

Since we weren't allowed to cross the street yet, we did it Mom's way.

Mom always tells me
how difficult my birth
was. I don't remember
enough to give

my side

of the story.

We were never permitted to talk back to Mom. No wonder she was always right. That's like having a debate where one team has to wear duct tape over their mouths.

It's hard to get
justice from a woman
whose role model is
JUDGE ROY BEAN.

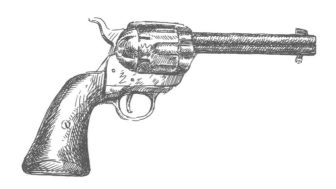

Mom never cared about justice. She cared about

PEACE AND QUIET.

As kids, our constant
battle cry was
"That's not fair."
Mom's response was
"I'm your mother,
not the
Supreme Court."

Being a mother is the most beloved adversarial position in the world.

We kids always complained, "But that's not fair."

If my mother had been fair, my homework would still not be done.

I was a troublesome child.
Mom told me when I
was finally allowed to go
out alone, she wondered
whether she should sit up
and wait for me to come
home or whether the
family should move and
not tell me where.

Mom, you
remember my
teenage years.

They were the ones right
before your hair turned
gray and Dad went bald.

Mom, you did make one mistake: you started looking younger than me.

A mother's three main duties are to love her children, to protect her children, and to embarrass them whenever the opportunity presents itself.

Mom was very protective.

I got my driver's license two years before I was allowed to cross the street by myself.

I was thrilled the first time I was allowed to wear long pants. It was when I rented a tuxedo for my

WEDDING.

Mom always taught us,
"Never talk to strangers."

I went through four
years of college and
never spoke to any of
my classmates.

Mom stressed it constantly: "Never talk to strangers . . . never talk to strangers . . . never talk to strangers."

I think Mom secretly wanted all of her kids to become mimes.

Mom, you always insisted that we never talk to strangers.

When you brought my new baby brother home from the hospital, I never said a word to him until we were formally introduced.

Once i got rebellious and daring: i actually spoke to a stranger. He didn't answer me, though. Apparently, his mother was as protective as mine was.

When Mom finally told me where babies came from, I was shocked. Every time I asked Dad, he just said,

"From North Dakota."

Mom actually convinced
me that the stork brought
me. That explained my
long nose and the fact
that I could fly.

Mom kept our
house spotless.

I was fourteen
years old before I
saw my first dust.

We never had ants
in our kitchen. That's
because Mom made
them all wipe their feet
before they came in.

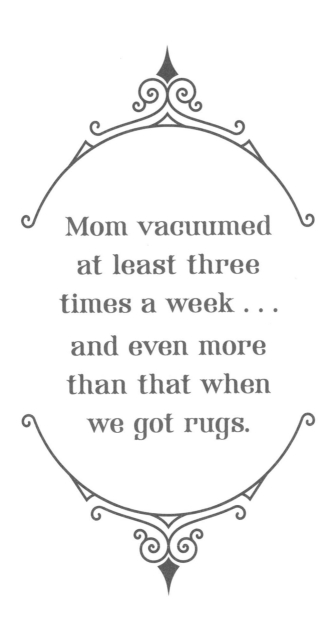

Mom vacuumed
at least three
times a week . . .
and even more
than that when
we got rugs.

A mother's love is unconditional, but don't for a moment think that means she's a pushover.

Mom is sweet, gentle,
caring, considerate.

That's because
she takes all her
animosity out on

FELLOW DRIVERS.

Mom drove us to school, to recitals, to soccer practice, to Little League games, to swimming lessons, to the dentist, to the doctor.

Once I told Mom I was going to run away from home.

She said,

"finally! A place where i won't have to drive you."

MOTHERHOOD
is always evolving.

The first ten years,
Mom is your
biggest fan.

During the teen years,
she's your worst enemy.

Then, in adulthood,
somehow she
becomes your
best friend.

My mom maintains that there are some things a mother doesn't need to know. Thank goodness, because i have a whole list of things i wasn't going to tell her.

I knew I was getting old when my mother stopped referring to my age in

MONTHS.

Mom, you loved me through all the phases I went through and even a couple that you went through because of the ones I went through.

You loved me
when I was good
and you loved me
when I was bad,
even though you
and I didn't always
agree on which
was which.

MOTHER,

you taught me right
from wrong.

Sometimes I couldn't
sit down for a few
days after the lessons.

You loved me even
when we didn't see
eye to eye.

Of course, it's hard
for me to see eye
to eye with a person
when I'm bent over
her knee.

Mothers
are a special kind
of angel—one who
cooks and does
dishes, too.

Mom, you won all the arguments with us over the years. Now we're sending in the second wave—the grandchildren.

Mom, you wanted
us to be good
all the time.
We compromised.

We agreed to be
good whenever you
were looking.

Mom, you always told us you would love us no matter what. Boy, talk about being handed a

BLANK CHECK.

Mom, I've watched you bending over a hot stove all your life. Someday I'm going to get you a taller stove.

Mother made all the rules in our family.

She was also the only one who kept them.

Mom had a place
for everything and
everything was in
its place.

The only problem was
that she could never
remember where those
places were.

Whenever i asked my mother for money to buy candy, she always said the same thing: "find my purse."

That was a no.

Ninety-nine percent of the time, Mom knew when I wasn't telling the truth . . . which, coincidentally, was ninety-nine percent of the time.

It was Mom who first
suggested that I get
my own apartment . . .
when I was five.

My mother had the patience of a saint.

It was Saint George, the one who slayed the dragon.

Mom always
taught us to
tell the truth.

Except when the
landlord knocked at
the door to collect
the rent.
Then she said,

"Tell him i'm not home."

Mom made sure that
I played soccer and
Little League.
She insisted I join the
church choir. She signed
me up for dance classes
and art classes. She
wanted me to be active
in the Scouts.

Then it dawned on me . . .
she just enjoys driving.

Mom, you always taught me those things that i shouldn't do.

Now that i'm over thirty, can we move on to those things that i *can* do?

Mom was always
overly protective.
Our sandbox had a
LIFEGUARD.

Mom, you always
encouraged me that
I could do whatever I
wanted to do.

However, you were
the one who decided
what I wanted to do.

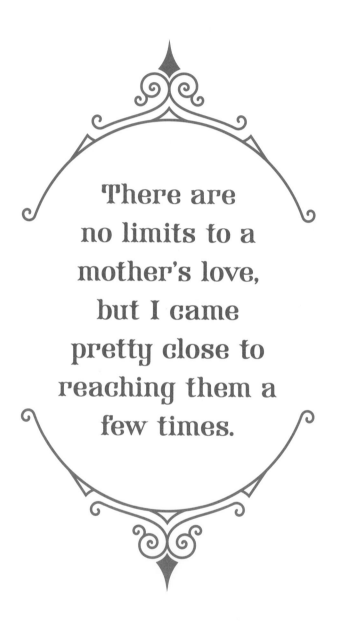

There are
no limits to a
mother's love,
but I came
pretty close to
reaching them a
few times.

Mom could lay down strict, unyielding rules, or she could offer loving, maternal advice. They were the same thing.

How could such a strict mother turn into such a forgiving grandmother?

We used to make breakfast in bed for Mom every Mother's Day. Mom would have to work like crazy to get the kitchen cleaned up in time to fix dinner.

Mom, remember
the time I made you
breakfast in bed
for Mother's Day?
It was great fun.

The firemen could
hardly stop laughing.

One Mother's Day, I tried to surprise you with breakfast in bed. But the smoke alarm went off and ruined the surprise.

Mom never used

BAD LANGUAGE

in the house.

She saved it up for
when she was driving.

Mom did a good job
of raising all of us . . .
even though we
had her

OUTNUMBERED.

Every day, Mom would put a note in my school lunchbox telling me how bright a child I was. I cherished those encouraging notes, but I managed to flunk geography anyway.

She should have put the notes in my geography teacher's lunch.

Nothing makes you appreciate your mother like becoming one yourself.

I never fully
appreciated my mom
when I was a kid.
Now that I've become
a parent, I wonder,
*How the heck did
she do it?*

One nice thing about
being a mother is
that you never have
to worry about what
to do with your

SPARE TIME.

Mom taught us right from wrong.

She was right; we were wrong.

My mom never said
"No" to me. But

"We'll see"

served the same
purpose.

Mom often mistook
me for a piece
of masonry.

"What am i talking to?
A brick wall?"

Mom always made
me eat everything on
my plate: "Children are
starving in China."

Now all the Chinese
people I see are skinny,
and I have a pot belly.

Whenever I came home with a black eye, Mom would scold me for fighting. But I know that inside she was hoping that the other kid looked worse.

Mom, you taught me
to be a responsible,
upstanding, hardworking,
dedicated, intelligent,
honest, principled,
virtuous, moral human
being. But then you made
one mistake:

You let me go to college.

Mom, I tried to be loving,
loyal, and your best
friend . . . but it was
making the dog jealous.

Mothers
are fully deputized
assistant guardian
angels.

Mothers are fearless.
They're the

TEXAS RANGERS

of parenting.

Mom had a surefire way of knowing when we were up to no good. She just checked if we were AWAKE.

My mother had

one

favorite child.

It was each
one of us.

I was a clever child.

I could always trick my mother into letting me do anything she wanted me to do.

Mom, whenever we disagreed, you always turned out to be right.

That's an awful lot of lucky guesses.

i thought you were always right because you were my mom. But now i'm a parent, and i haven't gotten

ANYTHING

right yet.

Mom, you taught
us the three great
Commandments:
love God, love one
another, and get
your elbows off
the table.

Anytime I cried, you'd say,

"i'll give you
something to
cry about."

I never understood
that. Wasn't it obvious I
already had something
to cry about?

Mom, after I straightened my room, did my homework, brushed my teeth, washed behind my ears, combed my hair, flushed the toilet, jiggled the handle, and practiced my piano lessons, I didn't have any time left for a CHILDHOOD.

I couldn't wait to be eighteen. I would be a responsible adult. Finally, I would be able to

play ball

and run in the house.

Mom always wanted me
to be a doctor, a lawyer,
or a clergyman.

I just wanted to be
what I was:

A LITTLE BRAT.

Mom used to read to me at bedtime. When i was a toddler, she read me

fairy tales;

when i was a teenager, she read me the

riot act.

Mom is an angel with knitting needles instead of a harp.

Mom showed her love for me by constantly knitting me sweaters.

I showed my love for Mom by occasionally wearing them.

Mom was always handy with a needle and thread. I was the only player on our football team who wore an embroidered uniform.

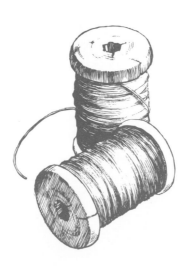

Mom had lots of
regulations.

If my mom had been in
charge of things, the
Ten Commandments
would originally have
been published as a

three-volume set.

When we disagreed with Mom, she always explained her point of view. It seemed the explanation always involved a wooden spoon.

Mom always said my room was a mess, and she was right. When I finally did get around to cleaning it, we found a pet dog we never knew we had.

My mom's a

SUPERMOM.

In fact, one year for
Mother's Day, we kids
wanted to buy her
a cape . . .

She turned that idea down.
She thought it might make
her look "hippy."

When we were kids, Mom
always insisted that
we do chores.

i've got good news for you,
Mom: i plan to finish mine a
week from next Thursday . . .

My husband has
promised to help me.

mom,

remember what you said to me when I went off to college? You said,

"Either clean up your room before you leave or take it with you."

Mothers have to
be suspicious,
skeptical, dictatorial,
stern, unyielding,
and relentless
disciplinarians.

It's great training
for becoming a
mother-in-law.

Mothers are precious. That's why God limited them to one per customer.

Mom, you were always
nice to my friends, which
was very charitable
of you because even
I couldn't stand some
of them.

Mom always said
she hoped one day
I would have a kid
just like me. I always
thought it was a
compliment.

Now i know better.

Mom got me a
SMARTPHONE.

She said, "I'll know where
you are at all times in case
you get into trouble."

I said, "Mom, if you know
where I am at all times,
I won't be able to get
into trouble."

As a kid, in the supermarket I liked to yell "Mom" at the top of my lungs . . . just to see how many moms I could get to turn around.

It was amazing; you were usually the only one not to.

MOM,

you taught me many things. I wish you had taught me sooner that the cat's tail is *not* a handle.

But Mom, I taught
you which size toys
would not flush down
the toilet.

Mom, you raised
your children in a
haunted house.

Every time something
broke in our house,
nobody did it.

For a woman who claims she's not my maid, Mom sure spends a lot of time worrying about how clean my room is.

Mom wasn't the best cook.

i was twelve before i realized
SYRUP OF IPECAC
wasn't a dessert.

Mom could make everything taste good. She said it was because she added a secret ingredient:

LOVE.

I found out later it was really

Cheez-Whiz.

Moms have many talents. For example, my mom can juggle more than any circus clown.

Mom, I still remember
when you would
lovingly sing me a
lullaby each night.

I would listen for
a while and then
pretend to fall asleep.

Mom did
have a favorite child,
but most of the time
it wasn't one of hers.

i won't go so far as to say
Mom is my favorite parent,
but she's definitely in the

TOP
TWO.

Actually, the best
advice I ever got
came from my dad.
He said,

"Listen to
your mother."

ABOUT THE AUTHORS

GENE PERRET has been a professional comedy writer since the early 1960's. He began his television writing career in 1968 on *The Beautiful Phyllis Diller Show*. Since then he has written or produced many of television's top-rated shows, including *Laugh-In* and *The Carol Burnett Show*. During his career, Gene has collected three Emmys and one Writers Guild Award.

Gene also worked on Bob Hope's writing staff for twenty-eight years, becoming the comic's head-writer and traveling to several war zones for Hope's iconic Christmas shows.

Today, he teaches classes in comedy writing. His hobbies include painting, sketching, and playing the guitar. He paints rather well, sketches adequately, but you don't want to listen to his guitar playing. No one does.

LINDA PERRET followed in her father's funny footsteps and sold her first professional joke in 1990.

Since then, she's supplied one-liners and comedy bits for Terry Fator, Bob Hope, Phyllis Diller, Joan Rivers, Yakov Smirnoff, Jimmie Walker, and other stand-up comics.

Linda was a staff writer for the television Emmy Award–winning special celebrating Bob Hope's 90th birthday: "Bob Hope—the First 90 Years."

She has cowritten two collections of business jokes, published by Prentice Hall—*Funny Business* and *Bigshots, Pip-squeaks, and Windbags*. She is the author of HMO's, *Home Remedies and Other Medical Jokes*. Her material has been quoted in *Reader's Digest,* the *National Enquirer*, and *Arizona Highways*.

Linda also launched a joke service called Perrets' Humor Files and continues to operate a newsletter for comedy writers and performers.

ABOUT FAMILIUS

Visit Our Website: www.familius.com

Join Our Family: There are lots of ways to connect with us! Subscribe to our newsletters at www.familius.com to receive uplifting daily inspiration, essays from our Pater Familius, a free ebook every month, and the first word on special discounts and Familius news.

Get Bulk Discounts: If you feel a few friends and family might benefit from what you've read, let us know and we'll be happy to provide you with quantity discounts. Simply email us at specialorders@familius.com.

www.facebook.com/paterfamilius

@familiustalk, @paterfamilius1

www.pinterest.com/familius

FAMILIUS

The most important work you ever do will
be within the walls of your own home.